MENTAL AND EMOTIONAL HEALTH IN CHILDREN

A WELLNESS PLAN FOR HOME AND SCHOOL

Conceptualized and written by
Kathleen A. Gallagher
MEd

With the support and business acumen and
leadership of Grace M. Collins, CADC

ISBN 978-1-64468-825-0 (Paperback)
ISBN 978-1-64468-826-7 (Digital)

Covenant Books, Inc.
11661 Hwy 707
Murrells Inlet, SC 29576
www.covenantbooks.com

To all children, that they may thrive with
mental and emotional health.

ACKNOWLEDGMENTS

I wish to thank all those people who helped me put this book together. First, I thank Chet Holden who did much to ready it for publication and kept encouraging me to bring it to completion. I thank Grace M. Collins, CADC; Mark P. Hannappel, PhD, licensed clinical psychologist; and Elizabeth P. Robinson, licensed specialist in child psychology for reading the manuscript and offering valuable feedback. I thank Carol Finney, for editing the manuscript, and Sandra Pratt, for her copying, faxing, and enthusiastic support.

CONTENTS

INTRODUCTION

Parents and teachers can have a profound impact on children merely by the way they speak and listen to children. Teachers and parents strongly wish children to live their lives fully and well. But few adults actually teach living skills at home or in school. Most young people flounder from ignorance of the skills never taught at home, school, or church. Adults attain much academic knowledge but often lack the management tools to handle their lives effectively. Teachers and parents often deal with children through automatic piloting, that is, by past conditioning from their own upbringing. Yet the messages many people got when they were children are ineffective or even harmful. Working with children today asks adults to broaden their perspectives, to be open to some nontraditional ideas, to form new beliefs, and to act differently from the past.

Parents often bemoan the reality that children come into the world without an instruction manual on how to raise them. Teachers get discouraged because they were not taught sufficient child psychology as preparation for their careers. And so this book will attempt to fill both voids and offer skills to anyone who interacts with children.

Results of living without having been taught life management skills:

1. People live by their wits. Energy for living and learning will be given to survival techniques such as perfectionism, people pleasing, trying to stay invisible, absence of healthy boundaries, and much guilt.
2. Young people become imprisoned by invisible chains which restrict happiness, learning capacity, and often a true ability to love.
3. Unsound messages going into a child's brain cause false thinking, leading to distorted feelings and negative behavior.
4. Years of developing unrealistic expectations of oneself and others will often lead to deep anger, violent outbursts, and some form of addiction.

CONTENT OVERVIEW

Chapters will expand on:

1. mini dialogues with children which will impart truths about human life and reality;
2. needed conversations between adults and children on how to handle circumstances in which they may find themselves;
3. language patterns and techniques for adults to use and avoid using when relating with children;
4. discussions with children about handling their emotions;
5. topics for creative writing to express a wide range of human feelings; and
6. wellness as connected with creating brain compatible environments so children can thrive.

Positive effects from learning life truths and sound living skills:

• Children become empowered with healthy thinking patterns.

- Mental health grows strong and often improves physical health as well. People of all ages act the way they feel and feel the way they think.
- Children experience a new happiness as truths of being human lead to new self-awareness of their own giftedness.
- Healthy persons love the pleasures of the mind and love to work.
- Addictions are often prevented. When the inner person is more satisfied and developed, the need for external, addictive pleasures is diminished.
- The informed child and later the informed adult will be more likely to make good choices.

What are life management skills?

1. Life management skills include learning about perfectionism, people pleasing, fear, and mistakes.
2. People live better when they can handle their moods of anger, sadness, worry, and loneliness.
3. They can choose wisely when they know their likes and dislikes and issues of power and control.
4. They live happier if they stay grateful and if they can apologize when necessary.
5. They will be freer when they learn how to say no.
6. They can engage in activities without guilt when they better understand the differences between introversion and extroversion.

CHAPTER 1

Mini Dialogues to Impart Life Truths

The following speech patterns between adults and children are casually dropped off in a non-lecturing way as opportunities present themselves. For example, at home, they can be passed along when getting ready for school, eating, driving in the car, watching TV, shopping, etc. In school, it works well to engage in a dialogue just before starting whole-class or small-group lessons. In the beginning, the adult does the talking for several weeks until children become familiar with the language. Within a short time, the pattern switches between a question and free-response answer, meaning children just call out a reply. The dialogues are meant to be ongoing as they usually only "click" with children when they face circumstances where the words offer a solution to a current life situation.

On Asking for Help

The adult says, "People are smart about different things. If another person knows something that you don't know, it doesn't mean that person is smarter than you. You may know something that the other person doesn't know. People are smart about different things. That's why it makes sense to help one another. I can show you what I know, and you can show me what you can do. So it's intelligent to ask for help."

In question-and-answer form, the dialogue goes like this:

Q: If you know something I don't know, does that mean you are smarter than I am?
A: No.
Q: Why not?
A: We are smart about different things.
Q: Why is it intelligent to ask for help?
A: Because we are smart about different things.

Regarding Mistakes

The adult says, "No one knows everything. It is because we are human beings, and that means we are limited. People can't be everything or do everything. They make mistakes because they don't know everything. People don't deliberately make mistakes. They happen because people are just learning how to live. Everyone can learn from mistakes so we don't make the same ones over and over again."
In question-and-answer form:

Q: Is it okay to make mistakes?
A: Yes.

Q: Why is it okay?
A: Because we are human…
    or we don't know everything…
    or everybody makes mistakes.

On Different Abilities

The adult says, "Some people are born with a talent for doing something special such as playing music or being artistic. Most people learn by trying something many times. This is called 'trial and error.' People make mistakes in the beginning and get better with practice."

In question-and-answer form:

Q: How do you get good at new skills such as playing certain sports, doing math problems, reading, or trying a new game?
A: By practice.
Q: What is making mistakes called when you are trying new things?
A: Trial and error.

On Learning

The adult says, "Each person has a time clock inside for when that person learns something new. If your friend learns something before you, it does not mean that person is smarter than you. Some people learn things fast, and some people learn after more days have passed."

In question-and-answer form:

Q: If someone learns something before you, does that
    mean that person is smarter than you?
A: No.
Q: What does it mean?
A: That person has a different time clock.

On Courage

The adult says, "It takes courage to live. It takes courage to try out for a ball team, a part in a play, or to say hello
to a new child in your class. Without courage, people have
few friends and a lot less fun in life. People grow courage
when they act in spite of their fears to try things that are
safe and good to do."
In question-and-answer form:

Q: When do you need to use courage?
A: When things are hard or when you don't know how
    it will turn out.
Q: Why is it good to practice using courage?
A: So you have more friends, or so you learn how to do
    more things, or so you can have more fun.

On Helping Others

The adult says, "It's okay sometimes to say no when
another child asks you for help. People cannot help everyone
all the time, or they don't get their own work done. If you say
yes all the time, you start to become angry because you are

not getting your own work done. If you never stop to help anyone, you may have no friends, and you become unhappy. So people say yes sometimes and no sometimes. If someone says no when you ask for help, just ask someone else."

In question-and-answer form:

Q: Is it okay sometimes to say no when another child asks you for help?
A: Yes.
Q: Why is it okay to say no?
A: I can't keep helping people when I'm not getting my own work done, or I just finished helping someone, and I need to get my own work done.
Q: Why is it wise to stop and help another person when we can?
A: Because helping someone makes us feel happy.
Q: What can you do if someone says no to you when you ask for help?
A: Ask someone else.

On One's Learning Timetable

The adult says, "It is okay to work fast or more slowly. It has nothing to do with your intelligence. The first one done is not the smartest. The first one done has a fast time clock. What's important is to finish what you start. Finishing things makes you happy."

In question-and-answer form:

Q: Is it better to work fast?
A: No.

Q: What is important when you are working?
A: Finishing.
Q: Why is it important to finish what you start?
A: Finishing makes us feel happy.

Who's the Boss?

The adult says, "You are the 'boss' of yourself. The only time I need to 'boss' you is when you forget to 'boss' yourself. Then it will be time to go to the quiet place until you get your power back."
In question-and-answer form:

Q: When does the teacher need to 'boss' you?
A: When I forget to 'boss' myself.

What Do You Like?

The adult says, "During your school day, try to remember the things you most like to do, what you prefer to do. Then think of the activities you don't like as much. You were born liking and disliking things. These are called your brain preferences. They help you decide what you might like to do as a job when you grow older or what people and hobbies will give you pleasure."
In question-and-answer form:

Q: Is it okay to have favorite school activities?
A: Yes.
Q: Why is it okay not to like everything?
A: Our brain was made that way.

Q: Why do you think people were made to have favorite activities?

A: So people will know what jobs and hobbies and people will give them pleasure.

Regarding Preferences

The adult says, "Some people are born who like to work alone most of the time. They are called introverts. Other people are happiest when they are with another person or group. They are called extroverts. Some people like to work alone part of the time and to be with others part of the time. All three ways are okay. Try to figure out what you prefer so you can pick jobs or hobbies or people that meet your preferences to be alone or with others. This will bring you happiness and pleasure in your activities."

In question-and-answer form:

Q: Is it better to like to work or play alone or is it better to like to work or play with other people?

A: Both ways are okay.

Q: Why are both ways okay?

A: Our brains were made to like different things, or we are born with preferences.

Regarding Choices

The adult says, "People have power to make many choices and decisions. This power is called 'free will.' But other people have 'free will' also and are able to make their own choices and decisions."

In question-and-answer form:

Q: What do you call your power to make choices and decisions?
A: Free will.
Q: What power do you not have?
A: The power to make choices and decisions for others when they are able to make their own choices and decisions.

Regarding Apologizing

The adult says, "When you hurt someone by what you say or do, it is important to apologize. Say 'I'm sorry I said that or did that.' Hurting anyone makes you feel sad and unhappy inside of yourself. Apologizing makes people feel better."

In question-and-answer form:

Q: Why is it important to apologize when you have hurt someone?
A: Hurting someone makes people feel sad and unhappy inside, or apologizing makes people feel better.

CHAPTER 2

HOME CONVERSATIONS BETWEEN ADULTS AND CHILDREN

Children need time, attention, and life-enhancing information so that they develop viable coping skills. This can release their motivation to learn and to live. Truth is freeing. When children are equipped with a healthy belief system, they come to understand they are not victims of circumstances. Rather they are active agents in the creation of their own lives.

Adults have the power and opportunity to fashion future generations of healthy people. The following at-home conversations are meant to be had with children at opportune times such as while eating a meal, helping with or checking homework, driving in a car, or saying goodnight in a child's bedroom.

On Making Mistakes

Being a human being is a great gift because it means we are never expected to be perfect. It means that we will make mistakes at times. Not having to be perfect is a great freedom. When we think we have to do something perfectly, it takes some of the fun out of things we are trying to learn. When we are afraid to make mistakes, we won't grow the courage to try new things. All we ever need to do is our best at that moment. If others don't like it, that's their problem, not ours. We keep getting better by practice.

On Ridicule

It's important not to laugh at someone when that person makes a mistake. Being laughed at is one of the things that hurts people and embarrasses them. It is a different situation when someone makes a mistake and says or does something really funny. Then we laugh because it's funny. We're not laughing at the person but at the funny thing that was said or done.

On Changing Other People

We can be a lot happier in life if we know we cannot change other people. I can only change myself. We change ourselves by the decisions that we make and by the choices that we make. Because we can't change other people, it's important to spend time with people whom we like and who like us.

On Practicing

When we practice something new over and over again, we usually get good at it. When we don't get better after a lot of practice, we may want to try something else. We are never good at everything. For example, we may never be a great ballplayer, but we are good at fixing or building things. Or we may not sing well, but we are talented at playing an instrument.

Regarding the "Right Way"

Some things may be right for you but not for someone else. There is not one "right way" for everyone except to do no harm. Do what seems right to you at the moment you do it.

Feelings Teach Us

All people feel happy or sad, glad or angry sometimes. All these feelings are our friends. They help us to know what to do to take care of ourselves. When you feel happy or glad, remember what just happened to give you that feeling. Then you will know whom you like to be with and what you like to do. When you feel sad or angry, those feelings will tell you whom you don't like to be with and what you don't like to do. Spend as much time as you can with people you like and doing things you like to do.

On Moods

It's important to know that you can't change other peoples' moods or the way they think. We each control our own moods and our own thinking. I can control my moods, and you can control yours. We can sometimes change a bad mood by eating some good food, taking a walk, riding a bicycle, or taking a nap. Sometimes it helps to think of what we are grateful for right now.

On Feeling Angry

If you ever feel angry because of what someone said to you or did to you, it's helpful to say right away, "I feel angry when you say that or do that." We usually can't stop the other person from what they say or do, but we can let them know clearly how we feel. Sometimes the other person will stop. Other times, they may not. Then it is up to you to walk away and stop spending time with that person. You have the right to be respected.

Fear Gives Information

Since feelings are our friends; feeling afraid is a healthy feeling. It tells us whom to be careful around and whom to stay away from. It tells us what to be careful of. New things can be scary to try, but if they are good things to do, we go ahead and do them anyway, and we are usually glad that we did so. But anyone or anything that could harm us is something to be afraid of and a reminder to stay away from that person or thing.

On Choosing Friends

Have you ever felt really happy when you're with some-one and you are laughing together?

These are the people to make friends with. Do not choose to spend time with anyone who says mean or unkind things about you. Choose friends who respect you because you are an okay person.

Thoughts Can Create Anger

It's hard to believe but no one else can make us angry. We make ourselves angry by the way we think. When we let someone make us angry, we give our personal power to that person. We may feel angry at what someone said or did but how long we stay angry is up to us. Because someone says something mean or unkind does not mean that person is right, or that what they said is true.

On Protecting Ourselves

Whenever we feel angry or afraid if someone has tried to touch our body in some way, it is important to tell an adult that we trust right away. When we talk about it, we may feel better, and the adult can help us. When we don't talk about it, it makes us sick inside, and that person may hurt us again.

On Meanness

It's okay not to like some people. It's okay not to like people who say you are stupid or too slow or who make fun of you or say you are not good enough. When people say mean things, it doesn't mean what they say is true. One great way to answer them is to say, "I'm sorry you feel that way." Then turn and walk away and go about your business. Refuse to have an argument.

Regarding Choices

One of the most special things about people is that we always have choices in every situation. We can choose our friends, and we can choose to be many different things when we grow up. It is important to choose work that you like because you will spend so much of your life doing it. Even when it looks as though you don't have a choice sometimes, you can always choose how you will think about a situation. You can choose to see the good side or the unhappy side of things.

On Introverts and Extroverts

Do you ever find that you don't like to do some things that other children like to do? That's okay you know. People like different things. One reason for this is that some people are born "introverts." These are people who like to do things alone. Other people are born "extroverts" which means they prefer to do things with other people most of the time. Both ways are okay. It's just one way in which people are different.

Be True to Yourself

Some of us are born with a liking to work and play alone most of the time. We will be happier being what we were born to be from the beginning. We don't have to try to be like other people. It's good to try new things, but one way is not better than the other. Be the way you are happy.

We All Have Talent

No one is more special or talented than someone else. Each person has different talents and weaknesses. By trying new things, we find what we are good at doing. Then we know the way we are special. Sometimes the way is how we care about other people. Sometimes it's a talent for creating something new. And sometimes it's a talent for teaching other people.

Having Different Opinions

It's okay to think differently from someone else. The way you think and do things may be the right way for you but not for everyone else. My way or your way is not the only way. It's okay for other people to think differently or to prefer to do things differently from you. This does not make them wrong.

We Can Always Learn

Life would be dull and boring if we knew everything about everything. There is so much fun in trying and discovering new things. If we think we are supposed to be good at something the first time we do it, then we may be afraid to try anything. There is something new to see and do all the time, even when we get older. Life can always be interesting if we want it to be.

We Are Responsible for Our Own Happiness

We each make our own happiness by the decisions that we make and by the choices that we make. No one else can make us happy. They may add to our happiness when we are with them, but we can still be happy when they are gone. No one can make us unhappy either. We may be sad because they are gone, but how long we stay that way is our personal decision.

On Listening to Others

Something that's important for our happiness is to know that we cannot change other people. If someone is sad or in a bad mood, we can say, "I'm sorry you are not feeling well," but we don't try to fix them and make them happy. Sometimes the loving thing to do is to listen to someone who is sad, but we cannot fix their sadness. We can say we are sorry they are having a bad day. That's all a friend can do.

On Apologizing

When we say or do something that hurts another person, it's important to apologize as soon as we can. When we don't, we grow sad inside. When we apologize, we feel happy again.

On Gratitude

Sometimes good things happen in our lives, and sometimes sad things happen. No one always has happy days. On sad days, we can choose people to be with or things to do that will help us to feel better. Finding things to be grateful for usually helps us to feel better.

On Avoiding Arguments

Sometimes another child tells you that you are wrong, but you do not think so. To avoid an argument, you might say, "Time will tell," and then say no more or walk away.

On Managing Homework

When you do your homework, start with a subject you like. This will give you energy. Then do the subject you like less or that you dislike or that you find difficult. Next, do something you like again. You put what you find hard between two activities that you like. This gets you through your homework easier, and you don't get so tired, or you don't feel grumpy.

People Are Different.

When we are born, our brains are created to find some activities easy and likeable and to find other activities difficult and stressful. We are not good at everything, but we are good at many things. We can get good at difficult things, but these activities will always cause us to get tired or irritable if we stay at them for a long time. Here are a few of the differences in people:

a. Some people like the schedule to be the same every day, and others want variety and a lot of change.
b. Some people may be good with technology, and others find it difficult.
c. Some people may be good money savers, and others are not.
d. Some people are born with a preference to work alone most of the time, and others like to be doing things with a partner or group most of the time. We can't change the way we are, and one way is not better than the other way. It's important to respect one another's differences and not try to change them.
e. These differences in people have nothing to do with our intelligence. We can be smart and not good at everything. Because we are good at different things, we need to help one another and be patient with one another.

Making Hard Things Easier

If you enjoy music, try playing music without words while you do tasks (school subjects or home chores) that you don't like or find difficult.

We All Can't Be Good at Everything

Take pride in what you enjoy and are good at. This is how you make your own happiness. Children who are good at other things are not better than you or smarter than you. They are different from you. You become unhappy and jealous when you always want to be good at everything.

We Have Different Ways of Learning

Some people learn better when they can *see* information on paper, a board, a chart, or a video. These people do well when they take notes. Other people learn better by hearing and listening to information. And still others learn by someone *showing* them one step at a time, such as how to use a new phone. All ways are okay. One way is not better then another. Your way to learn has nothing to do with your intelligence.

CHAPTER 3

LANGUAGE PATTERNS AND TECHNIQUES FOR SCHOOL AND HOME

Use *togetherness language* to foster cooperation.
For example:

- Let's take a look at page...
- Today's lesson is on page...
- Our work today is from...
- Let's start with number 4.
- It's bedtime now.
- Supper is ready, everyone.
- Can we stop now?

Use *neutral language* to create willingness.
For example:

- The lawn needs work. I could use your help. Will you help me?
- Let's wash the car and then play catch.

- How about we split some chores. (Name them.) What is your choice?
- Would you like us to work together?

Avoid *bossing language* which causes anger, fear, or rebellion.

For example:

- You need to stop that now.
- You should know the rule by now.
- You must start your homework now.
- You ought to know better.
- I want you to read ten pages.
- You need to know this by Friday.

Acknowledge what children do right or do well.

- In school, have children mark all their correct answers rather than checking their mistakes.
- Say to them, "Look at what you know today."
- And each day, you can learn something new.

Allow children to post their own work.

- Do this at home and at school.
- Invite them to do so if they wish.
- The adult does not select one child's work and not another child's.

Avoid public comparison.

- If a child gives an incorrect answer, the adult gives the correct one and doesn't call on another child.
- When possible, try to find something correct about the first response.
- For example: "Dallas is a city in Texas, but Austin is the capitol."

Make eye contact with every child every day at home and at school.

- Eye contact validates, affirms, supports, and nourishes self-esteem and a strong sense of belonging.
- Sustained eye contact can and does change a child's behavior from negative to positive.
- In school, it can be done as students enter at the classroom door or when collecting or checking classwork early in the day.
- At home, it could be as a parent sees the child off to school or wishes a child a good night's sleep.
- It is important that men give eye contact, as well as adult women.
- Some cultures have the tradition to always look down in the presence of an adult.
- However, in America, one cannot conduct business or grow strong self-esteem when two people won't look at each other.

After teaching something new or asking a question,

- end your sentence with such words or phrases as "okay?" or "isn't that so?" or "right?"
- After the child responds, then say, "What's okay?" or "Isn't what so?" or "What's right?"
- Have the children call out a response.
- When they can do this, they heard you.
- Example:
  o Adult: "No one can be good at everything. Isn't that so?"
  o Children: "Yes."
  o Adult: "Yes, what?"
  o Children: "No one can be good at everything."

Help children make choices, guide them with some boundaries.

- For example, at home:
  o "You can wear one of these three dresses or shirts."
  o "You can wear this or that pair of shoes, or you can do your homework in the kitchen or the den."
- And in school:
  o "You can choose your own partner." (Appointed partners may not enjoy working together because they are too different.)
  o "You can write a paragraph about your book, compose a poem about it, or draw and color a picture about it."

When a child is having trouble understanding

- First, say, "Let's take turns. I'll be first."
- Talk out loud about what you are doing as you take your turn. Then say to the child, "Your turn."
- If the child does not respond or does it incorrectly, take no notice and just say, "My turn."
- Again, talk aloud what you are doing and once again say, "Your turn."
- This is a way to reteach or teach a child while maintaining the child's self-esteem. Almost always, children will respond correctly before this process has been repeated ten times or less.

Work and pleasure are not opposites

- Never give free time as a reward and schoolwork as a punishment.
- Help children to see school as their office or place of work.
- Most of our lives are spent working. A healthy outlook encourages us to find satisfaction in and through our work.
- Children will dislike school when work is used to punish.
- People do need vacations and holidays to regenerate their energy. But when a child's goal is to work for free time, they cannot feel the pleasure of a job well done.

- A paycheck is a by-product for adult work, but it does not guarantee happiness if there is no pleasure in the job itself.

No external rewards

- When prizes, stickers, coupons, or special chores are given constantly to some children every day, these children lose touch with the greater reward— the pleasures of the mind and the satisfaction from stopping to help another person.
- Constant external rewards provide a "high" which developed over years can lead to wanting bigger rewards.
- This can lead to various addictions, which offer pleasure and satisfaction.
- Occasionally reward all the children for their hard work, courage, and willingness to help one another.

Never withhold love and affection to manage behavior

- Children need love as they need air to breathe.
- Without love and verbal approval, children can become people pleasers and perfectionists in their search for affirmation.
- People pleasers gradually lose their identity and can be easily controlled and manipulated.

Loving and respectful touch

- When at home, loving touch heals and comforts children and makes them think, "I count here."
- Patting, stroking, and hugging nurture children.
- Adolescents, especially boys, usually act embarrassed and push you away.
- Grin at them, ruffle their hair, and pat their shoulder anyway.

One-On-One time with children

- Greatly affirms them and helps to create healthy bonds between the parent and child.
- I know one father of five who takes them by turn out for breakfast on Saturday.
- Try to address some conversation to each child daily so they don't begin to feel invisible.

Children are taught to apologize if they have hurt someone.

- It is important that adults model this in their own lives.
- Apologizing makes us feel better on the inside.

Children need and want boundaries at home and in school.

- They feel safer with some structure.
- The best boundary is "respect the rights of others."

Too much competition is unwise with primary-aged children

- Their self-esteem and self-worth are just being formed.
- Until they grow awareness of their capabilities and have enough success in their young lives, losing triggers negative emotions.

Have a quiet place

- In school and at home where children can go to reclaim their power to "boss" themselves.
- In a calm voice, send children to that area.
- Let them know when you teach them about the quiet place that they can leave the area when they have "their power back to boss themselves."
- They may stay ten seconds, thirty seconds, two minutes, etc.
- The child must make a personal decision in order to leave the area.
- The adult makes no comment when the child leaves the quiet place.

At home, address individual attention to children.

- Solicit each one's opinions and preferences.
- Ask children what were the best and worst parts of their day.

Correcting children

- Prerogative of parents in their own home.
- When parents permit a behavior and a grandparent publicly criticizes it, parents need to support the children lest they feel betrayed.

Teachers should encourage every student

- Support their potential.
- By voice tone and kind eyes, let children know they are valued.

CHAPTER 4

DISCUSSIONS WITH CHILDREN ON HANDLING EMOTIONS

Purpose of Discussions

We teach skills for living by a process of simply listening to how others handle situations. We may think children should know better at certain times, but they do not unless they have been taught. Children act the way they have seen others act. And children act the way they feel unless they have learned other options.

When Discussions Are Used

In school, use a small-group time similar to a reading or math session with six to eight children sitting in a circle or around a table. At home, it can be a conversation at mealtime, while sitting in the den, playing a game, sitting with a child who is doing homework, or when getting ready for bed. It will work even with one child. In school, the discussion will take no more than ten minutes.

The Process

- Select a topic from the list provided below.
- Explain the procedure with such words as, "Today's lesson is about the feeling of anger. Feelings are our friends. They tell us what we like and dislike, whom to choose as friends and whom to stay away from. I'll mention one thing I do when I feel angry, and then each one of you can say something you do when you're angry, or it's okay to say, 'I pass.' Give each person your attention when it's their turn because they deserve that respect. It's okay for you to speak or not speak. No one has to talk. Let's not laugh at what anyone says because you know how you would feel being laughed at."
- In school, children from healthier homes will pass along healthy information. Children from less healthy homes will receive new information to broaden their perspectives.
- As you start off the discussion, share *one* of your own ideas or one of the suggestions offered below on that topic.
- Do not ask children to volunteer responses. Introverted or fearful children will not volunteer. When the group takes turns in order, more children usually take a turn.
- Do not use children's names. After one child has spoken or passed, just say, "okay, next."

- The teacher is the facilitator. Do not interact with any student no matter how wise or bizarre their comment may be.
- Let the group hear all the expressed options and form personal opinions about what has been revealed.
- At the end, the teacher (facilitator) does not prioritize the value of any comment given.

Topics for Discussion

The teacher takes the first turn and then says to the child beside her, "Okay, your turn." Try not to start with the same child each time.

Dealing with anger: *What can you do when you feel angry at someone?*

- If you can, say to the person, "I feel angry when you say that or do that."
- Walk away from the person or situation. Maybe the person is having a bad day.
- Tell a friend or an adult what you are angry about.
- Ride your bike or take a run.
- Stop and think before you do anything. You'll feel bad if you hurt someone back.
- Tell yourself some things you are grateful for.
- Go and do something you like to do.
- It's okay to feel angry. It's not okay to hurt someone when you're angry.

Bad moods: *"What can you do when you are in a bad mood?"*

- Eat some good food like peanut butter or fruit.
- If you can, take a nap. When you are tired, it's easy to get into a bad mood.
- Do something nice for another person.
- Do something that you really like to do.
- Make a list of what you are thankful for.
- Everyone gets in a bad mood sometimes.

Feeling happy: *"What can you do to help yourself feel happy?"*

- Finish something, a job, a chore, an assignment, putting something together, or fixing something.
- Help another person.
- Offer to play a game with someone.
- Make a gift for someone.
- Draw a picture and color it.
- Do something you like to do.
- Tell yourself all the things you are grateful for.

Appropriate fear: *"What is a good kind of fear? A good fear protects you from harm."*

- Fear that tells you to be careful because someone or something could hurt you.
- Good fear tells you to stay away from someone because they could hurt your body or say mean things that could hurt your mind.

- Good fear tells you where not to go because something bad could happen to you.
- Good fear tells you what not to do because you know it will get you into trouble like going far from your house without telling anyone where you are going.
- Good fear tells you not to take stupid risks that could get you hurt such as swimming when you are all alone or going far from home when you are alone.

Harmful Fear: *"What is a 'not good' kind of fear?"*

- Fear of trying something new even though it's an okay thing to do. Most people feel this kind of fear but go ahead and do the good thing anyway. The feeling of fear usually goes away once you begin to act.
- Fear of making a mistake. All people make mistakes while they are learning new things.
- Fear of what others may say although there's nothing wrong with what you want to do.
- Fear that you won't do something as well as someone else.

Responsibilities: *"What are you not responsible for as a child?"*

- Other peoples' bad moods and trying to make them feel better. You could say, "I am sorry you are feeling poorly."

- Other people's behavior. You don't need to apologize for something that someone else said or did like lying or cheating. You are only responsible for what you said or did.
- Taking care of adults who are able to take care of themselves.
- Making other people well if they are sick.
- Making other people happy. We are each responsible for our own happiness by our own choices.

More on responsibilities: *"What are you responsible for as a child?"*

- Schoolwork, homework, and chores around the house.
- Eating good food if you can.
- Keeping yourself as clean as you can.
- Getting enough sleep (nine to ten hours) so you have the energy to do your work during the day. Without enough sleep, you can get in a bad mood, and sometimes you become mean.
- Being the best person you can be each day.
- You are responsible for your feelings of anger, meanness, or jealousy. You are responsible not to hurt anyone by what you say or do when you have these feelings.
- You are responsible to make the best choices you know how to make.
- You are responsible to make yourself happy by the choices you make.

- Sometimes you need to be responsible for younger brothers or sisters if no adult is at home.

On feeling afraid: *"What can you do when you feel afraid?"*

- Talk to a parent or an adult at school and tell them why you are afraid. Some fears are good fears, and some fears are not. The adult will help you to know which it is. Fear of a person is usually a good fear, but fear of making a mistake is usually not a good fear.
- Stay near someone you trust.
- Say no to spending time with someone if you are afraid. This is a good fear to protect you. They may want you to do something that you know is wrong.
- Say no to going to places or doing things if you are afraid that you will get hurt.
- Never get into a car with someone you don't know or trust.

Being afraid to try new things: *What can you do if you are afraid to make a mistake? What if you are afraid to join a ball team or try for a part in the school play? What if you want to join the school band or just learn to play a musical instrument?*

- These are not good fears. It takes courage to live. Use your bravery and do them anyway.

- Most people feel nervous trying new things. These are good things to try, not hurtful things, so go ahead and do them. The nervous feeling usually goes away.
- If you get a "no" answer when you try to join a group, try something else. Remember, you grow bravery when you make the effort. It will be easier to ask next time because you will have more courage. Tell yourself all the things you are good at doing.
- Keep practicing the new skill you want to be good at. This will make you better at it.
- Remember, everyone makes mistakes. No one is good at everything. No one knows everything.

Making Yourself Happy: *What is something you can change about your life if you want to?*

- You can decide to do the best job you can each day.
- You can choose to think happy thoughts by thinking of things you are grateful about.
- You can decide to be honest by telling the truth and by not stealing.
- You can help to make yourself happy by doing something nice for someone else.
- You can speak with respect and kindness to people even when others do not.
- You can change the way you behave.
- You can decide to stop trying to change someone else. We cannot change other people.

On Changing Others: *What are things you do not have the power to change?*

- Making sick people well.
- Other people's bad moods.
- If other people don't like you even though you are a nice person.
- If people say mean things about you. Just because they say mean things, doesn't mean what they say is true. Sometimes you can just say, "I'm sorry you feel that way," and then walk away.
- Other people's behavior. You do not have to apologize for other people.

On Friends: *What kind of people should you choose as friends?*

- People who treat you with respect.
- People who tell you the truth.
- People who play fair.
- People who keep their promises.
- People who apologize when they hurt you. Don't keep them as friends if they keep hurting you in some way.
- People who like to do what you like most of the time.

On Feeling Lonely: *What can you do if you feel lonely and have to stay inside the house?*

- Play a game you can do alone.

- Make or build something.
- Draw in pencil or color.
- Read a good story.
- Listen to music.
- Make a card for someone.
- Write a story or a poem.
- Make up your mind that you can enjoy being alone.

On Gratitude: *Being grateful makes you feel good. What can you be grateful for?*

- Being alive with its many choices about what to do
- Food, especially your favorite food
- A bed to sleep in at night
- Friends
- Pets
- Toys
- Books
- Games
- Bicycles
- Sunshine
- Flowers
- Swimming
- Sports

On Being Proud: *What can you be proud of?*

- All the things you can do
- All the things you know

- That you can be a good friend
- That you are a good person
- That you do the best you can each day
- That you are responsible for your daily tasks and chores
- Helping someone
- Being kind to someone
- Forgiving people who say or do mean things to you. People say or do mean things when they are sick or unhappy

On Feeling Grumpy: *What can you do if you are feeling sad or are having a bad day?*

- Tell a friend what's the matter.
- Hug your teddy bear and sleep with it even if you are a teenager.
- Tell yourself, "This will go away, and I'll feel different tomorrow."
- Write down why you are sad even if you throw it away later.
- Do something you like to do.
- Watch a funny or favorite movie.
- Take a nap.
- Make a list of what you are grateful for.
- Everyone has bad days sometimes. Do not hurt anyone because you feel bad.

On Feeling Love: *What makes you feel loved?*

- Having a person hug you. Sometimes we have to ask someone to give us a hug because they don't know we need one.
- When someone says thank you to us.
- When someone says something nice about you.
- When someone pats you on the shoulder.
- When someone says good morning or good night to you.
- Having someone shake your hand.
- Having someone notice when you do something well.
- Telling yourself you are an okay person.
- When someone listens to you.

On Feeling Mean: *What can you do if you're feeling mean?*

- Stay away from people until you feel better.
- Take a nap. You may just be overtired.
- Tell yourself it's okay to feel mean, but you must be careful not to hurt anyone while you feel that way.
- See if you can figure out what caused the mean feelings. What were you just thinking about when you started to feel mean? For example, did someone say something nasty about you? Tell yourself that it isn't true. The person who said it was unhappy. It has nothing to do with you.
- Tell yourself the mean feeling will pass.

On Feeling Mad: *What can you do if you feel mad?*

- Tell someone what you're mad about and you usually start feeling better.
- You are sometimes mad because you want someone else to change their mind, and you can't change other people. You can change yourself though and what you want.
- If you're mad at another person, say to that person if you can, "I feel mad when you say that or do that." The other person may not stop, but you need to say something and then walk away.
- When you're mad, ask yourself, "How important is what I'm mad about?" Often it's not very important. So let it go and go on to do something else.

On Mistakes: *What can you learn from your mistakes?*

- Everyone makes mistakes.
- It's no big deal. Don't take it so hard. Tell yourself you are human and not perfect.
- If you learn something from the mistake, it was a good mistake. We often learn the right way to do something by making a mistake first.
- When you make a mistake, you are still an okay person. You are not a mistake.
- Say you are sorry if the mistake hurt someone else.

When Others Are Mean: *What can you do when some-one says hurtful things to you?*

- Just because someone says it, you don't have to believe it.
- Just because someone says it, doesn't mean it's true.
- Say to that person, "I'm sorry you feel that way." Then walk away and get busy doing something else.
- The person who hurts you is often a very unhappy person. Usually only unhappy people say hurtful things.
- If what the other person says hurts you, but it is true, then it is up to you to change your behavior.

Regarding Choices: *What choices do you have?*

- You are free to choose how to act.
- You are free to choose to have a good day.
- You are free to treat others with respect or not. When you don't, you will be unhappy.
- You are free to like what you like and like who you like.
- You are free to dislike some people, but you can still be kind and respectful to them.
- You are free to make your own happiness by the decisions and choices that you make.
- You can do what you feel is the right thing to do.
- You can pause and think before following anyone's suggestion.

On Boredom: *What can you do if you feel bored?*

- Listen to music while you finish the boring task.
- Ask someone to help you finish what is boring to you.
- If you can, stop what you are doing and go back to it later.
- Finish quickly what is boring and go on to something you like.

On Happiness: *Tell us one thing that makes you happy.*

- Open-ended responses

On Skills: *Tell us one thing you are good at either at home or at school.*

- Open-ended responses

CHAPTER 5

TOPICS FOR CREATIVE WRITING

Guidelines for Use

- In primary and middle school, after the phonics or English lesson, teachers might create a ten-minute creative writing time. It would allow children to get in touch with and express a wide range of human feelings. The length of the writing would be according to the grade level from a sentence to a paragraph. As an alternative to writing, children might have the choice to draw (illustrate) their response to the topic of the day.

- Choose *one* of the suggested topics. Vary between positive and negative emotions on consecutive days. Topics can be used more than once with a time interval.

- Use a special notebook so all the child's work is in one tablet. Much can be learned about the child when this writing is connected with the information on the *brain* discussed in chapter 6. Children can choose a notebook with colored pages which is a right brain preference.

Topics for Consideration

1. One of the best times I ever had was when…
2. It's always a good day for me when…
3. I feel afraid when…
4. I always smile when…
5. I remember feeling frightened when…
6. I had so much fun when…
7. I don't like it when…
8. The nicest person I know does…
9. Things that I feel sad about are…
10. I feel love when…
11. The meanest person I know does…
12. One day, I felt very happy because…
13. I feel very nervous when…
14. I laughed so much when…
15. I felt awful the day that…
16. Things I feel happy about are…
17. I felt so lonely the time when…
18. I feel helpful whenever I…
19. I felt so mad when…
20. I feel so grateful for…
21. I felt very angry one day because…
22. I like my best friend because…
23. I hated it when…
24. I jumped for joy when…
25. It was a big surprise to me when…
26. I was disappointed when…

27. I wanted to cry when…
28. I remember feeling worried the time that…
29. I felt proud when…
30. I remember how scared I felt when…
31. I like it when…
32. I remember how terrible I felt when…
33. Something I like to do outdoors is…
34. My favorite game is…
35. Something I like to do inside the house is…

CHAPTER 6

CREATING BRAIN-COMPATIBLE ENVIRONMENTS IN SCHOOL AND HOME

For our purpose here, a simple description of the human brain reveals four quadrants called frontal and basal left and frontal and basal right. Children are born naturally gifted in one or two of those modes. The other two can be developed, but their talents don't come naturally.

Inborn preferences are permanent and determine what we like to do versus what we can do. We can become competent in our weaker modes but prefer our natural modes.

Just by observing young children and what they gravitate toward or avoid, parents and early childhood educators can usually tell the dominant modes of a child. Then they can provide an environment in which a child can thrive. They will not force children into activities in which they have little seeming interest. Yes, we will want to expose children to developing skills in their weaker modes but not before we stand back and allow them to reveal themselves. Their self-esteem grows as they discover what they can do and what they know. Competency versus preference in life is not related to intelligence. They simply describe what we can do versus what we like to do. Children feel smart and energized when living in their dominant modes.

Following is a description of the characteristics of each of the four quadrants:

Frontal-left-brained children are naturally gifted in

- math,
- use of tools and machines,
- taking things apart and putting them together,
- logical analysis, and
- weighing and prioritizing.

In testing, the frontal left brain of children prefer multiple-choice questions because they can logically figure a response. Also they like to work alone and prefer images in black-and-white rather than color. They may come across as cool and distant because they dislike emotionality.

In classrooms, application could be that all children could choose to work alone or with another. Children quickly know who is good at what they do and choose those with whom they feel a compatibility. The classroom structure would allow for freedom of conversation while working. They would be free to choose their own partner or group for work. This structure enhances their pleasure in working. Also, frequently remind children at home and in school that it is intelligent to ask for help because we are smart about different things.

Basal-left-brained children are naturally gifted in

- preferring a schedule-and-daily routine,

- being attentive to details,
- being neat and orderly,
- holding on to large amounts of information,
- needing their "space" to be just so, and
- organizing, keeping, and locating records.
- Also, they require step-by-step instruction.
- They dislike spontaneity.
- They are thorough, slow, reliable, and methodical.
- They find change and interruptions stressful.

In testing, they prefer fill in the blanks and true-false tests because they have memorized many facts. Schools have been geared mainly to basal left-brained students with their preference for sameness. They are cooperative and enjoy the structure of a traditional classroom. It is stressful for them to share space with frontal right-brained children because they are so opposite in their living styles.

Frontal-right-brained children are naturally gifted in

- Creativity and innovation.
- They use imagination and intuition to solve problems. They know an answer but cannot always tell you how they know it or the process used to obtain it.
- They like change, risk, and variety.
- They are totally visual and prefer to keep all their things in piles where they can see them and not in a file cabinet or drawer.
- They possess strong spacial skills.
- They are inspiring, charismatic, and expressive.
- In testing, they prefer essay type questions.

Frontal-right-brained children's additional considerations:

- They test and challenge boundaries.
- They can inadvertently walk on people.
- They are restless, easily bored, and need to stretch and move to think.
- They do poorly with organizational requirements.
- Their work area usually looks messy because they pile things around them.
- They are delightful, spirit-filled people, but they are the hardest to satisfy in school.
- They comprise the most dropouts and behavior problems in a traditional classroom.
- They require a great variety of activities to hold their interest, and they cannot remain sitting at a desk for a prolonged period of time.
- They are more content if the classroom provides freedom of position and location while engaging in independent work and also plenty of choice.
- They are totally visual. They learn more by seeing than by listening.
- Having much information visually placed around the room aids in their learning.
- At home, there would be much friction if they had to share space with a basal left child because the two are so opposite.

Basal-right-brained children are naturally gifted in:

- These children naturally seek cooperation and harmony.
- They pick up nonverbal clues. They quickly notice when there is tension in the home and are the most damaged from a troubled environment.
- They value compassion and empathy and are the world's natural caregivers.
- They enjoy games.
- They are gifted with rhythm.
- They like bright colors.
- They like to "dress up" and change clothes frequently.
- Eye contact and smiles are important to them.
- They work for connections and good relationships.
- They are skilled at teamwork.
- In testing, they do poorly in multiple choice questions.

Basal-right-brained children's additional considerations

- They are poor money managers and spend impulsively. They are opposite to frontal left people who are skilled in finance.
- They often choose "peace at any price" and sometimes lose their identity in becoming "people pleasers."
- They find it extremely difficult to say no, lest they damage a relationship.

- They need to talk to learn. In school, these children thrive in a room where there is freedom of conversation while working.
- They are stressed by confrontation and misunderstanding.
- Teach basal right children that it is okay to say no at times. In school, if someone asks for help, you could say no because you have just helped two people, and you need to get your own work done. At home, for example, show children they can't help everyone all of the time without neglecting to take care of their own responsibilities.

Brain Strengths and Weaknesses

All people have a strongest and weakest brain mode. The weakest quadrant is diagonally opposite the strongest mode. If one's strength is frontal left, then one's weakest characteristics are in the basal right mode. If one's strength is frontal right, then the weakest mode is basal left. Reflecting on the descriptions of each mode will help to plan an environment which will enable each child to thrive. This knowledge will help to enhance a child's self-worth and self-esteem. Children's weak modes will then not be a cause for criticism, judgment, or insistence that children do better in certain areas. Children procrastinate when in their weakest mode. Staying in one's weakest mode without balancing it with one's strengths will over time create fatigue, illness, poor behavior, and depression.

Techniques to Help Students Manage Brain Weaknesses

- Sandwich an activity that you dislike doing in between two activities that you enjoy.
- Do something at home that you like to do. Then follow it with a chore you dislike. Follow that by something you do like, etc.
- In school, use freedom of choice frequently regarding independent work and teach children the sandwiching technique.
- Do two things at the same time. While doing something in your weakest brain, do something you like at the same time.
- While doing something you don't like, play music if you like music.
- When much of your day is given over to nonpreferred activity, have a hobby that greatly pleases you such as dancing, painting, belonging to a sports team, carpentry, skating, etc.
- Switch tasks with another person.
  - "I'll give the dog a bath if you clean our bedroom."
  - "I'll mow the lawn if you 'll help me with my math homework."

Introversion Versus Extroversion

Part of children's wellness includes recognition and acceptance of their introversion and extroversion needs.

- *Introverts* are energized by time alone and become irritable and discontent when they are forced into contact with others for a lengthy period of time. Their behavior deteriorates with too much togetherness. At home, introverts like to play alone or read. In school, it is helpful to give children the choice of freedom of conversation while doing independent work. Then they can choose to work alone or with a partner or group.
- *Extroverts* on the other hand are energized by much involvement with other people. With much aloneness or quiet, they daydream or fall asleep.
- *Some children are a balance* between introversion and extroversion. Others are heavily one or the other.

Learning Styles

In addition to strengths in one or two brain quadrants and an introverted or extroverted personality, children have a learning style as well. They are primarily a visual or auditory or kinesthetic learner. This means they learn best by seeing (reading) or hearing (listening) or touching or feeling or handling material.

BIBLIOGRAPHY

Benziger, Dr. Katherine, PhD, Thriving in Mind. *The Natural Key to Sustainable Neurofitness,* 2013. www.benziger.org

CURRICULUM VITAE

Kathleen A. Gallagher, MEd
500 Rockingham Ln, #312
Richardson, Texas, 75080
Home: 972-235-0397
Cell: 214-356-3457
kathleeng1024@gmail.com

Education

MEd, Tulane University, New Orleans, Louisiana
BS, Fordham University, New York

Competencies

The creation of home and school environments that ensure intellectual safety for all children.
Vast experience in teaching life skills and truths of human nature.
Knowledge in forming whole brain environments.
Conducting group sessions with students on topics of handling feelings and emotions.

Certificates

Merrill Harmin, Inspiring Strategies Institute
Katherine Benziger, Thriving in Mind
Sister Grace Pilon, Consultant for WORKSHOP
WAY®
State of Louisiana, School Administrator
State of New York, Teacher and School Administrator

Employment History

State Mentor for Region X and XI in Texas, Alternative
Certification Program (1995–1998)
National Consultant teaching Graduate Courses
and In-Services on Educational Topics and Wellness
Programs for Teachers and Students (1975–1998)
Administrator of the St. David WORKSHOP WAY®
School, New Orleans, Louisiana (1967–1975)
Classroom Teacher of Grades 4 to 8 in Louisiana and
New York (1953–1967)

Awards

25 Years of Service to The Workshop Way, Inc.

ABOUT THE AUTHOR

Kathleen A. Gallagher taught elementary and middle school classes for twelve years. She then administered a school in New Orleans, Louisiana, that had been beset with extreme behavioral problems. Using a program called WORKSHOP WAY®, the difficulties almost completely disappeared as students developed a love for learning. After receiving her BS from Fordham University, Kathleen earned an MEd from Tulane University. From 1975 onward, she was an education consultant providing courses and in-services on effective techniques and wellness programs for teachers and students.

Now retired, Ms. Gallagher writes of her experiences so that other educators will find help and empowerment. You will want to read her other book already published named "Freedom to Thrive-A Pathway to Intellectual Freedom" It shows how every student can be mentally safe in every classroom.